DIGITAL CAREER BUILDING™

CAREER BUILDING THROUGH

USING MULTIMEDIA ART AND ANIMATION TOOLS

MARCIA AMIDON LUSTED

ROSEN
PUBLISHING®

New York

Published in 2014 by The Rosen Publishing Group, Inc.
29 East 21st Street, New York, NY 10010

Copyright © 2014 by The Rosen Publishing Group, Inc.

First Edition

Library of Congress Cataloging-in-Publication Data

Lüsted, Marcia Amidon.
Career building through using multimedia art and animation tools/Marcia Amidon Lusted.
        pages cm.—(Digital career building)
Includes bibliographical references and index.
  ISBN 978-1-4777-1725-7 ((library binding))—ISBN 978-1-4777-1743-1 ((pbk.))—ISBN 978-1-4777-1745-5 ((6-pack))
  1. Commercial art—Vocational guidance—Juvenile literature.
  2. Commercial artists—Vocational guidance—Juvenile literature.
  3. Animators—Vocational guidance—Juvenile literature. I. Title.
NC1001.L87 2014
741.6023—dc23
                                                                    2013015015-

Manufactured in the United States of America

CPSIA Compliance Information: Batch #W14YA: For further information, contact Rosen Publishing, New York, New York, at 1-800-237-9932.

CONTENTS

CHAPTER ONE

FROM PENCIL TO STYLUS

Not so long ago, people who were involved in creating illustrations, graphic art, and animated films relied on methods that had been used for decades. For illustrations and graphic art, they used canvas or paper and drew their art using pencils, ink, paint, charcoal, and other types of traditional artists' tools. Comic books and graphic novels were painstakingly drawn by hand with pencil, inked in to provide outlines and details, and then colored. These pieces of art were pasted on a layout board and photographed. The film was turned into a printing plate that ultimately printed the book. The same basic method was used to print posters, flyers, or magazine pages. It was a very mechanical, messy process involving knives, rubber cement, and solvents to attach the art to the layout board and then to make any subsequent changes or adjustments.

Animated film was an even more complicated process. First, a paper storyboard was created for the film. Drawn in pencil, it mapped out the film's different scenes with rough artwork showing what they would include. Then all the frames of the film had to be drawn by hand as individual cels. A cel, short for celluloid (the material that animated images were once drawn on), was one particular drawing of a character, which would be laid over a static background. The drawing of the character was done in ink on one side of the cel, and it was colored in with paint on the opposite side. Cels were

Animators used to rely on traditional art techniques like drawing and coloring images on celluloid. An artist in 1940s Hollywood shows hand-drawn cels ready to be photographed.

generally drawn by senior animators. The number of cels required for an animated sequence depended on how much movement or how many different versions of a character were needed. Less experienced junior animators drew scenes that filled in between the character action cels, to create the story sequence. With each second of animated film consisting of twenty-four frames of film, a huge amount of hand drawing was necessary just to create even a short cartoon. Each cel and background drawing also had to be hand-colored, usually by junior animators. Only by involving many different animators at many different skill levels could a film be completed in a reasonable amount of time.

Enter the Computer

Today many of the traditional art methods have been set aside for faster, easier, and more efficient methods. For the most part, this is thanks to the invention of the computer. The personal computer has been around since only about 1974, when Intel marketed the first small, home-sized computer, the Altair, as a $400 kit. The Apple II, as well as PCs marketed by IBM, Commodore, Xerox, and Tandy, followed. Instead of the massive computers of the early twentieth century, which required entire rooms to house them, people could now have small, affordable computers in their homes—and use them to create art.

Now very few artists and art designers can do their work without computers. In 1987, the Adobe software company released a program called Illustrator. It not only allowed artists to do typesetting on a computer, but

Computer software programs such as Adobe Illustrator first allowed artists and designers to create and manipulate images digitally.

it also included the ability to create and manipulate shapes. It was the first time that designers and artists could use digital tools to create precise layouts and logos. It also allowed illustrators to create artwork using a computer, instead of creating physical artwork and then photographing it for use in magazines or other media. In addition, it allowed graphic designers to manipulate photographs, improving them or eliminating unwanted elements, and to create new photographs by adding and combining existing images.

Starting in the nineties, instead of photographing physical layouts and sending them to be made into printing plates, designers could send a portable document file

Snow White vs. Toy Story

In 1937, Walt Disney released the first full-length cel-animated feature film, Snow White and the Seven Dwarfs. Many of the animators who worked on the movie were not professionally trained artists but instead had worked as newspaper cartoonists. The Disney studio held classes for these animators, focusing mainly on anatomy and movement, taught by professional artists. The movie required 1,500,000 separate drawings in both color and black and white and took four years to complete. It even required the creation of a new type of camera with eight decks so that various action and background cels could be stacked and photographed in different degrees of focus.

Compare this with the 1995 Pixar film Toy Story, the first feature-length animated movie created entirely by computer. It also took four years to create, but the bulk of the animation took only six to eight months; the rest of the time was spent in development. Twenty-seven animators worked on Toy Story, using four hundred computer models to animate the characters. Once they created the models, the animators added computer coding for motion and articulation. The character of Woody alone required over seven hundred coded motion controls.

Every shot in the film passed through eight different teams. These included the art department for color and lighting; the layout team, which decided which models to use in each shot; and animation, which created the characters and then compiled the shots. The final animation step was a computer process that rendered each shot into a completed form. In total, Toy Story required eight hundred thousand computer hours to render all the animation shots.

Pixar's *Toy Story* was the first feature-length film animated entirely using computers.

(PDF) quickly and easily. A PDF could be easily shared among people with different computer systems and software, and corrections could be made fairly easily.

Computers and Animation

Computers also made the process of film animation much easier and more efficient. In fact, computers brought about new styles and techniques in both animation and regular moviemaking. As early as 1969, scientists were creating computer programs designed to make animation easier. These programs helped animators create the drawings that filled in the film sequences between the key drawings of the senior animators. By using a computer to fill in these images, instead of the lengthy process of having junior animators draw them, there could be a better sense of movement to the story. Software designers created a program that could take the key animation cels and use them to generate entire film sequences.

Computer animation continued to develop, and now entire movies are made with computer-created images. Pixar's *Toy Story* (1995) was the first feature-length animated movie made entirely with computer-generated animation. Disney and Pixar developed their own animation system, called the Computer Animation Production System (CAPS). It combined software, scanning cameras, computer workstations, servers, and even custom-designed desks to replace the traditional methods of inking, painting, and post-production for animated films. Today, animation is rarely done using cels. Disney's animation studios stopped using cels in 1990, once they started using CAPS instead. Computer animation programs now make it possible to create the extremely realistic animated characters in movies such as *The Polar Express* and *Avatar*.

 Want to see a demonstration of how background animation was created for Disney's *Snow White and the Seven Dwarfs*? See a video demonstration at http://www.youtube.com/watch?v=W4vrAysxWuY.

Animation programs and the use of computers also led to the development of computer-generated imaging (CGI). This technology enables live-action moviemakers to create realistic special effects much more cheaply and easily than they could using models or special effects makeup. It has allowed them to create effects that would not have been possible in the past, such as the dinosaurs in the *Jurassic Park* movies and extreme stunts and character effects. The first use of CGI was in the original *Star Wars* movie in 1977. It was used to create the 3-D trench on the Death Star that Luke Skywalker maneuvers through during the movie's climax.

A New Generation

Many of today's professional artists and graphic designers have never experienced what it is like to create and design without the use of computers. They have grown up with the technology, as well as new genres for digital animation, such as computer and video games. Many first learned about multimedia art and animation tools by using the ones available for home and personal use. Several of the best computer software programs for computer animation, such as Maya and 3D Studio Max, have been made available in reduced-price educational or learner's editions for home use. With a computer and a drawing tablet, many teens have been able to start learning computer animation as a hobby. There is a wide range of software that hobbyists use, including LightWave, Houdini, Hash Animation: Master, and Pixar's RenderMan.

USING MULTIMEDIA ART AND ANIMATION TOOLS

 Remember, buying animation software for your home computer works only if your computer has the ability to run that software, so make sure it has the necessary requirements, such as the correct operating system, speed, and graphic ability. You can usually find these listed in the information about the software.

Teens have been able to use digital art tools on their home computers for fun and as a stepping-stone to a career. However, digital artists are usually regular artists first, learning the basics of drawing and painting in the traditional way. People interested in computer design or digital art have been able to build on those art skills and learn design programs such as Photoshop.

For teens who are interested in the field of multi-media art created with digital tools, learning these skills can pave the way to some of the most exciting careers in digital art and design.

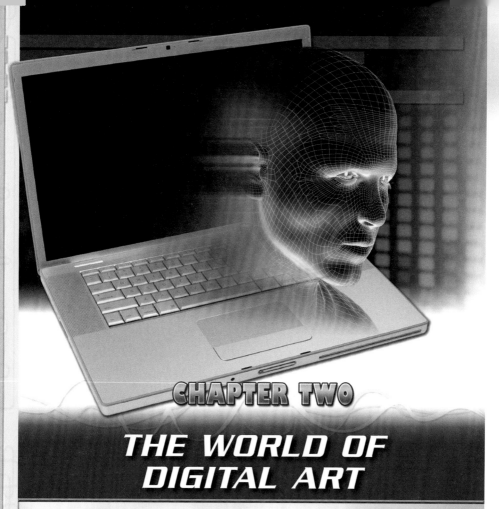

CHAPTER TWO

THE WORLD OF DIGITAL ART

Digital art is a field that is not very old, but it is evolving rapidly as the power of computers and their applications in art and graphic design expands. For those who are interested in working in the fields of digital art, design, and animation, what kinds of jobs are available?

From Cartoons to Video Games

Once upon a time, animation was limited to cartoons, including children's television cartoon programs, short features, and feature-length movies. All of these mediums still exist in the twenty-first century, but there are new mediums as well, especially in the video game industry. According to the U.S. Department of Labor's

Occupational Outlook Handbook, multimedia artists and animators is a job category that is expected to grow by 8 percent between 2010 and 2020. Most of this is due to the increasing demand for animation and computerized special effects in movies, television, and video games.

Computer animation jobs have common elements, even if they are applied in different mediums. Animators create graphics and animation using computer animation and drawing tools. They often work on teams with other animators on projects such as movies or video games. They may also do research for upcoming projects in order to create realistic designs or animation or create storyboards for new films or games. These storyboards map out the key scenes in a film or a game before the real work of animation begins. Animators may edit finished animation sequences after receiving feedback from directors, game designers, or other clients. They may also do administrative work, such as meeting with designers and directors to plan upcoming projects, create timelines, and set deadlines.

Animators may also specialize within the field. Some may excel at creating realistic characters and movements in a film or a game, while others are best at creating settings and backgrounds. Video game animators also specialize within their category. For example, some may focus on designing different levels for a game, while others concentrate on the game's look and feel. Often, many different team members produce pieces of a project, such as a game or animated film, and then these pieces are put together to create the finished product.

Some video game animators excel at creating realistic characters, while others are good at creating settings and backgrounds.

Lots of Flash

Computer animators are in demand for Flash animation. This is the kind of animation often used on Web sites, multimedia formats such as CDs and multimedia presentations, and e-mail content and banners. Flash animators work closely with creative directors in charge of advertising to create animation that complements the design and style of advertising materials. They can work for advertising agencies, public relations companies, marketing firms, Web and graphic design companies, video gaming companies, and educational publishers and media. This career area is expected to grow by 14 percent over the next five years, as companies are using increasingly realistic and engaging images to promote their products.

A related field requiring multimedia art and animation skills is software development. Companies that create software for various applications often need computer-animated images or sequences for their products. In educational software, for example, companies may create games or activities for children that use computer graphics and animation to make them interesting and engaging. Even software programs for adults often require animation for interest or clarity.

Movies and More

Other multimedia art and animation careers focus on creating the special effects that have become increasingly important in live-action feature films.

Tools of the Trade

What are the most common tools and technology used in a multimedia art or animation career?

- *Personal computer*
- *Panoramic digital camera*
- *Graphics tablet*
- *Digital paper and digital pen (to save handwritten text in a digital form)*
- *Computer-aided design (CAD) software, such as Autodesk Alias*
- *Software for developing digital environments, such as Adobe AIR or Unreal Engine*
- *Graphics or photo imaging software, such as Adobe Illustrator or Corel Painter*
- *Video creation and editing software, such as Adobe Director or Apple Final Cut Studio*
- *Web platform development software, such as Microsoft Silverlight*

Computer-generated images (CGI) are a cost-effective way to create live-action effects without the need for stunts. CGI can include using live actors to create computer-generated images of stunts, appearance effects, or other unusual elements that actors cannot do on their own.

CGI is also used to create exotic or fantastical locations in movies, which are then incorporated into live-action scenes. This saves moviemakers the cost

The 2009 movie *Avatar* used both live-action and computer-generated characters and settings.

of constructing expensive sets or traveling to difficult locations for filming. CGI is used in both movies and television, as well as in commercials.

Print and Digital Publishing

Finally, multimedia artists and animators are needed in the publishing industry. Not only can they use software and digital art techniques to create e-books and online magazines, but they can also use modern computer animation and art skills to make traditional publishing easier. Animators work on graphic novels and comic books as well as magazines and illustrated books, and many of these mediums use computer art and animation skills. They are used for layout and design, including tweaking images and photographs to better fit the design of a particular page or to edit out unneeded elements. They are also used for transferring traditional art to the printed page through scanning.

What are the types of graphic software most often used in publishing? Adobe Photoshop, Photoshop Elements (a less expensive version of Photoshop), GIMP, and Corel Photo-Paint are all used for editing images.

A Day in the Life

But what is it really like to work in the multimedia art industry? There are many different types of settings, from offices to working from home, but most jobs have common elements.

Animator Chris Chua works as an animator for Disney's Pixar Studios. His interest in animation started when he was a child and loved animated movies and cartoons. His career began as a character layout artist for Matt Groening's animated television show *Futurama*. He then worked on animated feature films for DreamWorks, such as *Sinbad* and *Flushed Away*. Since joining Pixar, he has worked on movies such as *WALL-E*, *Up*, and *Brave*. He also mentors animation students.

In an interview with the Web site Animation Career Review, Chua stressed the importance of learning traditional art skills before becoming an animator. He said, "I've been very passionate about drawing since I can remember. I encourage all my students to get a sketchbook and draw as often as they can, no matter what their skill level is. It helps you start a regimen of observing people and capturing something about them that interests you. It really helps me as an animator when I can pull from direct observation and put it into a scene that I'm animating."

He also talked about finding inspiration from master animators. Growing up, he said he was "absolutely obsessed" with the work of American animator and illustrator Glen Keane, who worked on many classic Walt Disney animated features. "I would watch his scenes over and over on video, study his drawings in my collection of 'Art Of' books, and even tried to draw like him! I just loved his relentless drive to breathe as much life as he could into his characters...I'm *still* in awe of his work to this day!" Chua urges students who are interested in animation not to wait until college or the workplace to create their own short animated films.

 CHECK IT OUT You can read more of Chris Chua's interview at http://www.animationcareerreview.com /articles/pixars-chris-chua-discusses-day -life-animator-and-how-he-got-there.

Working in the gaming industry is also a career with growing popularity among students, especially those who grew up playing computer and video games. Nate Torkildson, a 3-D artist with Red Monkey Games and Gamer Salvation, was able to turn a childhood dream of video game design into a career reality, partly by getting started on his career early on.

 Hands-on, traditional art skills and techniques are still important, even for those who are interested in digital art and animation.

On the Web site of the Digital Media Academy, he said, "I've dreamed about making games since I was seven years old. I think I still owe my parents about a million dollars in quarters from many visits to the arcade long ago. During my teenage years, I became serious about pursuing a career in design within the gaming industry. I've always been creative, but I wanted to take my skills to the next level. I enrolled in creative and technical courses...to transform my passion into a solid skill set."

Torkildson continued to focus on video game design after high school. He earned a degree in computer science from the University of Washington and studied 3-D animation and visual effects at the Vancouver Film School. He said, "After graduation, I was looking for my first big gig in the gaming industry. But, like all new grads, I had to prove myself. I worked tirelessly to build my own video game to give my potential employers a taste of what I could do."

Torkildson admitted that the video game industry is fast-paced and demanding and requires long hours, often on nights and weekends. There is constant competition as many people are eager to enter the field. He said, "People have this fantasy that working in the gaming industry means you'll play games all day. This isn't the case."

Careers in the multimedia art and animation fields are competitive. Even though jobs are expected to increase at a faster rate than in many other careers, many people are interested in them. So what can someone do to get started on the path to one of these careers, even before it's time for higher education?

CHAPTER THREE

STARTING FROM HOME

Many teens like to play with multimedia art and animation tools, from the simplest apps available on a smartphone to the most expensive animation software available for home use. Teens are now spending more time using computers and digital media than ever before, and they have more opportunities for sharing their creations every day. But there is a big difference between creating animation, art, and illustrations with a computer for fun, and pursuing it with a career goal in mind. If teens find that they are serious about digital art as a possible career, how can they take these casual hobby skills and start paving the way for the future?

Getting Started

Of course, the first step for anyone interested in multimedia art or animation is to become familiar with the tools used in these fields, and then become adept at using them. There are many types of digital art and animation software that can be used at home and are affordable for students.

Digital art software comes in two versions: 2-D and 3-D. Two-D is basically the digital version of drawing on a flat surface by hand. Three-D means that not only can artists create an image in two dimensions, but they can also view it from other angles and animate the image. Three-D software allows digital artists to create characters, architecture, landscapes, objects, and special effects as well as flat images.

 Many sites review and compare the different types of animation software available, for instance http://3d-animation-software -review.toptenreviews.com.

Beginners should start with simple software, some of it available free online, to learn the basics of drawing digitally. Basic 2-D drawing programs include Gimp, Corel Draw Graphics Suite, Painter, and Photoshop. Basic 3-D software includes Blender, LightWave, and Carrara 8 Pro.

Three-D software can also be purchased for specialized applications, such as landscaping or creating characters. These programs are optimized to do a particular task more easily and quickly than in an all-around 3-D software program. Landscaping 3-D programs include Bryce 7 Pro, Terragen, and E-on Vue. Character creation 3-D programs include DAZ Studio and Poser.

The most important thing to remember about any type of digital art software is that it takes time to learn to use the program well. But once you learn to use the software tools in one program, it will be easier to use them in others.

Digital artist Dawid Michalczyk said on his Web site, "Be prepared to spend long hours with the software you choose to learn. Start small, and gradually and steadily improve your skills. Concentrate on fundamentals—learn the basics first. Focus on building a solid understanding of how the software works." He advises aspiring digital artists to buy an introductory book or to use the software manuals if they are well written. He also recommends

It takes time and practice to master multimedia art hardware and software.

looking for help on the Web through forums, FAQs, Usenet, and tutorials.

In addition to getting art and animation software for practice at home, there are many places that offer classes in digital art tools. Larger high schools may offer courses as part of their art or computer curriculum. Many teen centers, community continuing education providers, art studios, and colleges may also offer multimedia art and animation classes that anyone can take. Such classes are a good way to get started with learning software and techniques under the guidance of someone who is familiar with them. They may make it faster and easier to become adept with these tools.

Developing a Body of Work

Once users become familiar with the tools of digital art and animation, they can begin using them to create artwork, illustrations, or animation to showcase their skills. The goal is to create a body of work—such as a collection of digital artwork or short animated films—in order to be able to show what they have accomplished and what they are capable of. This becomes a portfolio, which is a collection of work that can be shown to a potential college, employer, or client to demonstrate an artist's ability and skills.

The quality of the artwork or animation in a portfolio will probably change over time as a teen becomes more adept at the skills and tools needed to create digital art. That's why it is so important to constantly practice and create digital artwork. Hopefully, one's technique will improve and the finished pieces will get better and better. Over time, a teen should create a large collection of completed work so that he or she can choose the best of it for the portfolio.

 Before you post any of your work online, be sure to read any legal information or disclaimers for that site, such as privacy policies, rules for the use of your work, and copyrights.

What kinds of things should be part of a multimedia art or animation portfolio? It depends on your interests and your goals for a career. A traditional artist or animator might have a collection of physical work, such as paintings, sketches, or a graphic novel, that can be carried around and handled. A digital artist or animator is more likely to have more of a mixture of mediums in his or her portfolio. It might still include physical works, like a graphic novel, a comic strip, or a piece of writing with digitally generated illustrations. It might include printouts of digitally created art. However, the portfolio would also include work that is only accessible digitally. This could include an animated or CGI video, a short demonstration of a video game or a particular setting or character, an e-book, or even a Web site with graphic elements created by the artist.

Portfolios can also include real-world examples of a teen's graphic art skills, such as posters, brochures, or other artwork created for school, a local business, or a nonprofit group. When trying to enter the field, creating art or animation for exposure and experience is just as important as being paid for that work. The more

The Warning

One piece of advice that teens hear constantly is that they should be very careful about what they post online. As soon as you click the upload button on a photograph or a video, you have no more control over it. That embarrassing video of you and your friends at a wild party or a photo that you thought was incredibly funny when you were twelve could still be out there, shared with other Facebook friends or uploaded to a Web site in another country. This could be the case even if you think you deleted it. You might think the item is gone, but someone might have saved it or passed it on, and a potential college or employer who searches on your name might find it. Employers and college admissions officers are getting more and more adept at finding this kind of information. This warning may be even more important for potential digital artists or animators, who are likely to post their work on Web sites, YouTube, blogs, and other public forums. The best rule of thumb? Don't post anything, no matter how good you think it is, that you wouldn't want a parent, teacher, or employer to see.

examples of your skill and talent you have, the better off you'll be when it's time to create your portfolio. As you begin to create work for a future portfolio, think about creating a variety of work that will not only show off what you do best but also show that you are versatile and can do more than one type of digital art well.

What's So Important About a Portfolio?

Constantly practicing multimedia art and animation skills, and learning how to be good at them, is the first

These characters are the work of a student at New York University's Center for Advanced Digital Applications and were included in the student's portfolio.

step to a career in this area. Doing this with an eye toward assembling a portfolio is the second step. But why will a portfolio be such an important part of the process?

Just as musicians have auditions to show how strong their musical skills are, digital artists have a portfolio to show potential schools or other training organizations how good they are. A portfolio is useful first in applying to college and may even be a requirement for admissions consideration. A portfolio is also useful when a student already in college wants to apply for an internship with a film company, ad agency, publisher, or other organization that uses digital art in business applications. It may also be extremely helpful when it's time to find a job in the industry, since it shows an employer what skills and abilities a prospective employee has.

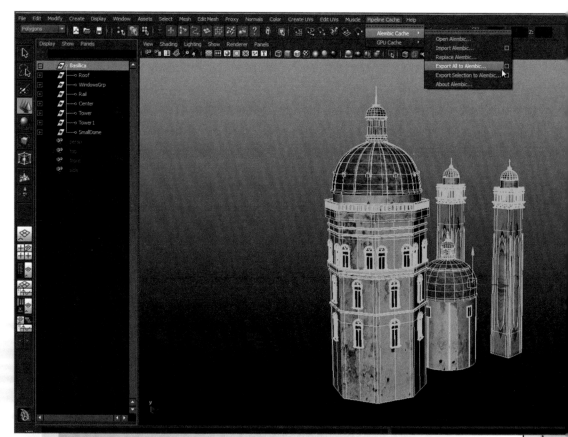

Digital design software can be used to create structures and settings for graphic art and movies.

Basically, the road to a career in digital art or animation begins with becoming familiar with the necessary tools and then continues with constant practice. Over time, by saving all of their work, prospective digital artists can not only build a solid portfolio of finished work to show colleges, employers, or clients, but they can also see the progression of their own abilities over time. These are the first steps along the path to a career in one of the many fields that rely on digital artists.

CHAPTER FOUR

MAKING A PLAN

At first, teens with an interest in digital art will spend most of their time and energy simply thinking about the artwork itself. They will work on mastering the tools and developing their technique—and perhaps their own distinctive style and artistic imagination as well. But in order to move ahead with a career in multimedia art or animation, at some point it is important to narrow the scope by setting a specific career goal. And to do that, they need to know just what their options are.

Working in Multimedia Art or Animation

There are many different jobs that fall under the category of multimedia art and animation. Some of these job

 Digital art software and tools like drawing tablets and styluses are often used to create illustrations.

titles, such as graphic designer, art director, creative director, and animation director, are broad. These professionals may perform many different tasks and work as one of a team or in a supervisory capacity. The first step is to decide what specific area of multimedia art you are interested in. Then you can explore the job possibilities within that special category.

Artists who are interested in being illustrators have many choices, including becoming a graphic designer or graphic illustrator. Graphic designers use computers to create drawings in 2-D and 3-D, often for advertising campaigns or Web sites. Traditional art techniques may be employed, and they are combined with special digital techniques to create multimedia campaigns. They often create the interactive art features in a Web site design. A graphic designer may focus on both a print marketing campaign and a Web site, creating a theme and making sure it is carried out in all mediums. Graphic illustrators may illustrate traditional media like books, comic books, or magazines, but they create them using digital tools. There are even more specialized illustrators who create illustrations for medical and scientific purposes.

Animators' jobs vary according to where they work and how complex the company's organization is. A large company such as Pixar may have many teams of computer animators, whereas a smaller company may have just a few people to produce their animation. The same is true of companies that produce digital special effects for movies. There may be large teams or just a few people in these jobs. An animation director or a television or film content producer oversees the work of the animators, 3-D artists, or visual effects artists. In most cases, entry-level jobs will be as assistants to more experienced animators or visual effects artists. As a person's expertise increases, he or she is given more responsibility and can move up the ladder to do more complex work.

When it comes to creating content for video games, jobs tend to be divided according to the expertise of the developer. Some specialize in character creation and others in settings, for example. They work under the supervision of the overall interactive content or game developer, who conceives the entire vision of the project and coordinates all the different aspects of the game.

There are, of course, other job possibilities under the overall category of multimedia art and animation, and it often depends on the workplace. Chances are that you can determine which aspect of art or animation you find most appealing and begin setting goals with that career in mind.

Setting Goals

Once you have determined your overall goal, such as working as an animator for a major animation film company, then you can begin to break it down into smaller goals. For example, you might decide that your dream job is to work for Pixar Animation Studios. Your first goal is to become familiar with the kinds of animation software you are likely to encounter in a large film company. Your next step might be to find some courses in your high school or community in order to add to your skills. You will have to make a choice about

Taking courses in digital art while still in high school is a good step toward a multimedia art career.

education, too, once you are approaching high school graduation. Will you go to a traditional four-year college or an art school?

Once you are enrolled, you might consider finding an internship with an animation company, perhaps even Pixar itself. Internships are valuable not only for the real-world skills they teach but also because they help you create contacts that may help you get a job. They also provide immersion in the job and can help you determine if the career you're interested in is really for you.

 Pixar has a section of its Web site just for internship opportunities: http://www.pixar .com/careers/Available-Internships.

As you set goals, consider all of the skills you need to have for your potential career, in addition to the technical skills related to computer systems and software. For example, if you are interested in working as a graphic designer in the publishing or advertising fields, you will need to have basic knowledge of communications and media production. You may also need customer service skills, such as meeting quality standards and meeting the needs of clients. As a designer, you'll certainly need to be familiar with design techniques and principles. Similarly, if you are interested in becoming an illustrator, you need basic knowledge of fine art theory and techniques.

Of course, you need to know the basics of computers and other electronics, beyond just the software programs that you might need for art or animation. It is

More Than Skill

One misconception about computer-generated art or animation jobs is that they don't require artistic talent. It is true that someone who is good with technology, adept with computers, and able to learn software can create basic images or animation even if he or she isn't particularly artistic. But most companies who hire digital artists are looking for more than just technical skill. They are seeking potential employees who are good artists first and know how to use technology second. Talent is still important, even in the realm of computer art.

also vital to have a solid command of the English language, including spelling, grammar, and vocabulary. Many of these skills—such as communication skills, English, and computer skills—are ones that you can work on while you are still in high school.

What School Is for Me?

The question of where to go for higher education, and what kind of degree to pursue, is always a tough one. But if you are interested in multimedia art and animation, you have even more choices. You can choose to go to a traditional four-year college or university and major in art, or possibly computer design or animation, if they are offered. Or, you may choose to attend a school that specializes in art or in design and technology. These schools offer majors in specific areas such as game design, multimedia and Web design, and computer animation. Some art schools offer general graphic design majors with a specialization in print or Web design.

How do these options differ? Art schools tend to focus more on studio work, or the creation of artwork. On the other hand, a traditional college's art program might include a great deal of art history and other academic courses. The choice of a school and a program depends on your career goal: If you want to be a traditional artist who just happens to create using multimedia tools, you may want to pursue an art degree at either a college or school of art. If your focus is purely on video game design, you may want to attend a school that focuses on computer design and technology and offers a specific game design major. Talking to some people who work in your target career, such as family friends or people in your community, can help you determine the best option.

 Your high school guidance counselor can help you explore different options for colleges and schools in this field.

Because multimedia art and animation relies so heavily on technology and skills, most employers prefer that job applicants have a college or art school certificate or degree. It is still possible to be hired without a degree and learn on the job, but it is less likely than in the past. Ideally, you can combine academic studies with on-the-job training by doing internships with companies while you are still in school.

Once you have decided what kind of school you want to attend, you will need to do your homework in

A student explores g-speak, a spatial operating environment with a glove-based gestural input system. It is one of the newest technologies for creating digital content.

terms of deciding where to apply. You'll want to create a list of possible schools and determine what they have as admissions criteria. If a school requires you to take certain high school courses before you can apply, then the time to learn this is now, when you still have enough time left to take those classes. Many art schools and art programs require a portfolio, which you have already been thinking about and collecting work for.

Once you have established goals for yourself, the last key piece is to reflect on your skills and work and build your portfolio.

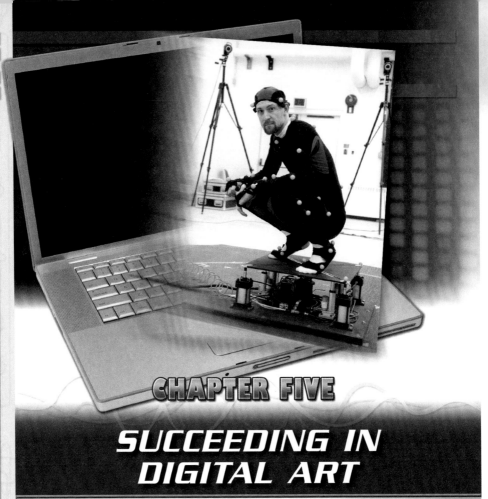

CHAPTER FIVE

SUCCEEDING IN DIGITAL ART

You've got a goal, and now it's time to do one of the most important things to get you there. It's time to show what you can do and create a portfolio. You already know that a portfolio is an important method for showing what you can do, either for admission to a college or other school, or to show a potential employer. But how exactly do you take your existing body of work and turn it into a package that you can use?

One Media or Many?

Traditional artists who are seeking careers have to decide whether to create both an online and a print portfolio. But in the fields of multimedia art and animation, it goes

An online portfolio is a must for anyone seeking work in the fields of multimedia art and animation.

without saying that an artist must have a digital portfolio in addition to a print one.

Some multimedia artists do not even have a print portfolio, such as artist and blogger Alex Mathers, who told *Digital Arts* magazine, "I've found success as an illustrator without ever requiring the use of a print portfolio. I have received a substantial amount of work via the Internet, and it was through having a well-designed online portfolio that enabled clients to see what I could produce." However, other artists believe that a print portfolio lets a potential client see what your work looks like in print. So especially while you are getting started, having both versions of a portfolio is the best way to go.

For more tips on creating an effective art portfolio, see http://emptyeasel.com/2007 /10/11/how-to-prepare-an-art-portfolio-a -guide-for-freelance-and-self-employed-artists.

Another question is whether artists should display their work on a dedicated Web site that belongs solely to them, or as part of a larger Web site that exhibits the work of many different digital artists. Illustrator Ben Tallon told *Digital Arts*, "[Community] sites...are great for extra exposure, but it's essential to have your own island on the Web. It looks professional, it's your official show-case for what you do, and it's very rare that clients will take a chance on you when you're buried under a thou-sand other creatives on a portfolio site."

 You can see Ben Tallon's online portfolio at http://bentallon.com.

What to Include

Obviously, you want to include your best work in any kind of portfolio, but how do you determine just what this is? First of all, study the portfolios of other digital media artists, either on their Web sites or, if you know any artists personally, in print. Note what kinds of work the artists include and how they organize their Web site or portfolio booklet. Does the print version have an interesting cover or binding? Is the artwork appealing? It may be worthwhile to have your work printed or pho-tographed professionally, so that your portfolio is not just a collection of printouts from your home computer.

If you're not sure how well you've presented yourself in your portfolio, ask for feedback from a teacher or design professional.

It should also be in a format that enables you to add and subtract work in the future. Then, as you begin creating more professional work, you can highlight what you have done for clients.

Remember, one way to build your body of work and fatten your portfolio is by doing free or low-cost work for local clients. A Web site that you designed for a local nonprofit organization, a poster you created for a local theater group, or even an animated film that you made for a school film festival are all good additions. Contests are another good way to get your work out into the public eye and create different pieces for your portfolio.

If you aren't sure how well you've represented yourself in your portfolio choices, ask for professional feedback from a teacher or an artist working in the same field. He or she can help you decide what best shows your talents, skills, and accomplishments.

Looking at Jobs

You've assembled a great portfolio. Once you've completed your higher education, you'll be looking for your first job in the field of multimedia art and animation. What is the best environment for getting your start?

Six Tips for an Online Portfolio

In an interview with Digital Arts magazine, artist Alex Mathers shared six tips for designing an online portfolio site:

1. *Keep the design clean and simple, but incorporate items, such as a logo, that highlight your identity.*
2. *Make sure your best work is immediately visible.*
3. *Continually update the site with new work.*
4. *Avoid small thumbnails.*
5. *Don't make navigation within the portfolio challenging for the viewer.*
6. *Make sure your online portfolio is compatible with mobile platforms.*

If you are interested in working in graphic design in an advertising agency or publishing environment, you can start out with just your college or art school degree and a solid portfolio. You have the basic skills, and the rest will come through on-the-job training once you are creating digital media related to products and services.

Careers in animation or movie special effects are more likely to be environments in which you begin at an apprentice level and work your way up to more responsibility and creativity. Some experts contend that the film industry is one in which a formal college degree is not that important, and skills and industry knowledge are the keys to getting a job. They urge students to get apprenticeships and internships working with real movie professionals, in order to build networking connections and accumulate the skills they need to get a permanent job. Others, however, say it is important for job seekers to have a college degree to show that they have studied the field thoroughly.

Jobs in film animation and special effects tend to be more difficult to get than jobs in Web site design or graphic art because there are fewer positions in this field and a lot of competition for them, and also because they tend to be limited geographically to places like California and New York. Web site design and graphic design, on the other hand, are occupations that are needed by many different types of businesses, all over the country.

Multimedia artists and animators also have the option of working as freelancers. This means that they are not employed by a particular company but work for

Multimedia art professionals often work together on projects.

a variety of different companies, usually on a contract basis. They might be given a certain job to complete or a certain project to work on for a limited amount of time. This is a good idea for people who like to have the freedom to work at home, to work only when they want to, and to do many different kinds of projects. However, freelance workers do not have the stability of a steady job, and they may find themselves going through periods of time without any work at all. It also means that they won't have the benefits—such as health insurance and retirement programs—they would have with traditional full-time employment.

Careers in multimedia art and animation and careers in graphic design are expected to grow over the next ten years. Digital animation will grow more slowly because there are fewer jobs in the field. There is also increasing competition from overseas, as many companies hire animators from other countries, such as Japan or China. Graphic design jobs are expected to grow more quickly than animation jobs because there are so many businesses and companies that require these services.

On the Job

What are the important things to remember once you have landed a job in the field of multimedia art and animation? Basically, they are the same as in any other

Members of the Disney features animation team collaborate during a meeting. Teamwork is an important part of many digital animation jobs.

workplace. Attitude is important, especially when starting out. Be willing to do whatever is asked of you, communicate in a positive way, and avoid criticizing or complaining about your work or your workplace. You will likely have deadlines for your projects and work, and it is imperative that you meet these deadlines. In many cases, other people will depend on your completing your work according to schedule so that they can complete theirs.

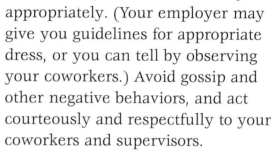

Professionalism is also important. Dress neatly and appropriately. (Your employer may give you guidelines for appropriate dress, or you can tell by observing your coworkers.) Avoid gossip and other negative behaviors, and act courteously and respectfully to your coworkers and supervisors.

Teamwork is also important, since most art and animation jobs involve working with others to complete a larger project. This means not only getting along with other team members but also fulfilling your responsibilities to make the team function smoothly.

Finally, once you have achieved a career in your field, that doesn't mean you stop growing in your skills and abilities. You will most likely have formal on-the-job training as well as informal education as you work and learn. You may also need to take further classes, particularly if you are working in computer design and need to stay current on software and other technical aspects of the job. Your employer may pay for further training, or you may have to do it on your own, but it is important to stay up to date in your field.

It is very possible to take a hobby or interest you have as a teen in high school, and through hard work, build those hobby skills into a real career. And chances are, if you find a career in something that you are naturally interested in, it will be a satisfying and enjoyable one for many years to come.

GLOSSARY

admission The process of entering or being accepted to enter a school, institution, or organization.

benefit A payment, gift, or service provided by an employer to its employees.

cel A transparent sheet of film material, such as celluloid, that can be drawn on and is used to create animation.

client Someone who uses the services of a company or a professional person.

compatible The ability of a computer to use software that was designed for another computer or digital device.

format The way something is arranged or set out, or the material it uses.

frame A single photographic image in a motion picture.

freelancer A self-employed professional who works for different companies on projects instead of committing to permanent employment with one company.

internship A program that provides a student or recent graduate with supervised training in a real-world work environment.

medium The material an artist uses to create artwork.

mentor To advise or train.

multimedia Using more than one means of communication, such as text, graphics, images, audio, and video.

navigation The act of moving purposefully within a virtual environment, such as page to page on a Web site or the Internet.

nonprofit A company or organization that is not set up to make a profit.

panoramic An unobstructed and wide view of an area in all directions.

PDF Portable document file; a file format that shows an electronic image of a text or text and graphics that can be viewed, navigated, printed, or sent.

platform The underlying computer system on which applications or programs run.

solvent A substance, usually a liquid, that can dissolve other substances.

storyboard A sequence of drawings, often including some directions and dialogue, showing the shots planned for a movie or television production.

stylus A pointed instrument used as an input device with a pressure-sensitive screen or tablet.

thumbnail A small image, often used as a preview of the larger version.

tutorial Instruction in how to use a computer system or software package, often built into that system or package.

FOR MORE INFORMATION

ACM Siggraph
c/o Association for Computing Machinery
2 Penn Plaza, Suite 701
New York, NY 10121-0701
(800) 626-0500
Web site: http://www.siggraph.org
ACM Siggraph is the Association for Computing
Machinery's special interest group on computer graphics
and interactive techniques. Its mission is to promote the
generation and dissemination of information on these
topics. It has both professional and student chapters, as
well as chapters in Canada.

AIGA, The Professional Association for Design
164 Fifth Avenue
New York, NY 10010
(212) 807-1990
Web site: http://www.aiga.org
AIGA is a global community of design advocates and
practitioners. It serves all types of designers and offers
student groups.

Graphic Artists Guild
32 Broadway, Suite 1114
New York, NY 10004
(212) 791-3400
Web site: https://www.graphicartistsguild.org

This group supports all graphic artists—including, but not limited to, designers, illustrators, cartoonists, animators, digital artists, and photographers—and works to raise standards for the entire industry.

International Digital Media and Arts
Association (iDMAa)
P.O. Box 622
Agoura Hills, CA 91376-0622
(818) 564-7898
Web site: http://idmaa.org
This organization serves educators, university scholars, and organizations with interests in digital media, as well as people currently working in the field. It is especially interested in how digital arts relate to other fields, such as the Internet, radio and TV, cinema and video, computer games, mobile computing, and more.

International Game Developers Association (IGDA)
19 Mantua Road
Mt. Royal, NJ 08061
(856) 423-2990
Web site: http://www.igda.org
The International Game Developers Association (IGDA) serves all individuals who create video games. The association is dedicated to improving game developers' careers and lives through community, professional development, and advocacy.

Toronto Animated Image Society (TAIS)
60 Atlantic
Toronto, ON M6K 1Y2

Canada
(416) 533-7889
Web site: http://www.tais.ca
This organization encourages the exchange of information, facilities, ideas, and aesthetics within Toronto's animation community. TAIS membership is made up of independent and professional animators, educators, enthusiasts, and artists. It has a specialized animation studio where animators and other artists can create independent animated work.

Web Sites

Due to the changing nature of Internet links, Rosen Publishing has developed an online list of Web sites related to the subject of this book. This site is updated regularly. Please use this link to access the list:

http://www.rosenlinks.com/DCB/MAAT

FOR FURTHER READING

Bancroft, Tom. *Character Mentor: Learn by Example to Use Expressions, Poses, and Staging to Bring Your Characters to Life*. New York, NY: Focal Press, 2012.

Byrne, Paul J. *Art Off the Wall: Computer Game and Film Graphics*. New York, NY: Heinemann-Raintree, 2007.

Facts On File. *Discovering Careers: Movies*. New York, NY: Infobase Learning, 2012.

Ferguson Publishing. *What Can I Do Now? Animation*. New York, NY: Infobase Learning, 2010.

Ferguson Publishing. *What Can I Do Now? Film*. New York, NY: Infobase Learning, 2010.

Furgang, Adam. *Internship & Volunteer Opportunities for TV and Movie Buffs* (A Foot in the Door). New York, NY: Rosen, 2012.

Gilland, Joseph. *Elemental Magic: The Art of Special Effects Animation*. Boston, MA: Focal Press, 2009.

Habgood, Jacob. *The Game Maker's Companion*. New York, NY: Apress, 2010.

MacLean, Fraser. *Setting the Scene: The Art & Evolution of Animation Layout*. San Francisco, CA: Chronicle Books, 2011.

Rauf, Don, and Monique Vescia. *Virtual Apprentice: Cartoon Animator*. New York, NY: Checkmark Books, 2009.

Rogers, Scott. *Level Up! The Guide to Great Video Game Design*. New York, NY: John Wiley & Sons, 2010.

Scholastic. *Hot Jobs In Video Games: Cool Careers in Interactive Entertainment*. New York, NY: Scholastic, Inc., 2010.

Solarski, Chris. *Drawing Basics and Video Game Art: Classic to Cutting-Edge Art Techniques for Winning Video Game Design*. New York, NY: Watson-Guptill, 2012.

Stoneham, Bill. *How to Create Fantasy Art for Video Games: A Complete Guide to Creating Concepts, Characters, and Worlds*. New York, NY: Barron's, 2010.

Stratford, S. J. *Field Guides to Finding a New Career: Film and Television*. New York, NY: Checkmark Books, 2009.

Tortorella, Neil. *Starting Your Career as a Freelance Web Designer*. New York, NY: Allworth Press, 2011.

BIBLIOGRAPHY

Amron, Mike. "Creating Computer Animation at Home." *Animation World Magazine*, August 1999. Retrieved February 20, 2013 (http://www.awn.com/mag /issue4.05/4.05pages/amroncgi.php3).

Bennett, Neil. "How to Build a Winning Portfolio." *Digital Arts*, June 15, 2010. Retrieved March 2, 2013 (http://www.digitalartsonline.co.uk/features /illustration/how-build-winning-portfolio).

Boglioli, Bonnie. "Pixar's Chris Chua Discusses a Day in the Life of an Animator and How He Got There." Animation Career Review, December 19, 2011. Retrieved February 24, 2013 (http://www.animation careerreview.com/articles/pixars-chris-chua -discusses-day-life-animator-and-how-he-got-there).

Boone, Andrew R. "The Making of Snow White and the Seven Dwarfs." *Popular Science*, January 1938. Retrieved February 13, 2013 (http://blog .modernmechanix.com/the-making-of-snow-white -and-the-seven-dwarfs).

Bureau of Labor Statistics, U.S. Department of Labor. "Multimedia Artists and Animators." *Occupational Outlook Handbook*, March 29, 2012. Retrieved February 24, 2013 (http://www.bls.gov/ooh/arts -and-design/multimedia-artists-and-animators.htm).

Burton, Michelle. "Flash Animator: Career Profile." Animation Career Review, October 5, 2011. Retrieved February 24, 2013 (http://wwwanimationcareer review.com/articles/flash-animator-career-profile).

Careers.org. "Occupation Profile for Multi-Media Artists and Animators." Retrieved December 29, 2012 (http://occupations.careers.org/27-1014.00 /multi-media-artists-and-animators).

Creative Skillset. "Jobs in 3D Computer Animation." Retrieved December 29, 2012 (http://www .creativeskillset.org/animation/careers/3D _computer/index_1.asp).

DegreeDirectory.org. "What Do Multimedia Artists and Animators Do?" Retrieved December 29, 2012 (http://degreedirectory.org).

Education-Portal.com. "Be a Multimedia Artist or Animator: Career Roadmap." Retrieved December 29, 2013 (http://education-portal.com).

Michalczyk, Dawid. "Digital Art Tools for Beginners." February 18, 2012. Retrieved February 24, 2013 (http://www.art.eonworks.com/articles/digital_art _tools_for_beginners.html).

O*NET OnLine. "Summary Report for Multimedia Artists and Animators." 2010. Retrieved February 24, 2013 (http:// www.onetonline.org/link/summary/27-1014.00).

Roberts, Tanya. "A Career as a 3D Artist." Digital Media Academy. Retrieved March 2, 2013 (http://www .digitalmediaacademy.org).

Walton, Kimberley. "How to Prepare an Art Portfolio: A Guide for Freelance and Self-Employed Artists." EmptyEasel.com. Retrieved March 3, 2013 (http://emptyeasel.com).

Webdesigner Depot. "Design Before Computers Ruled the Universe." February 29, 2012. Retrieved February 19, 2013 (http://www.webdesignerdepot.com).

INDEX

About the Author

Marcia Amidon Lusted is the author of 80 books and over 350 magazine articles for young readers. She is also an assistant editor for Cobblestone Publishing, a writing instructor, and a musician. She lives in New Hampshire. Working in publishing, she sees first-hand the work of digital designers and artists every day.

Photo Credits

Cover, p. 1 © iStockphoto.com/Andrea Hill; p. 4 (inset) mattus /Shutterstock.com; p. 5 © AP Images; p. 7 David Young-Wolff/Stone /Getty Images; p. 9 © Mark Richards/PhotoEdit; p. 13 (inset) design36/Shutterstock.com; p. 15 Gears of War® 2 image used with permission. © 2013, Epic Games, Inc.; p. 18 © 20th Century Fox /All rights reserved/Courtesy Everett Collection; p. 21 Jupiterimages /Brand X Pictures/Thinkstock; p. 23 (inset) Corepics VOF /Shutterstock.com; p. 25 Photononstop/SuperStock; p. 29 Center for Advanced Digital Applications–CADA/New York University /School of Continuing and Professional Studies; p. 30 © Autodesk, Inc.; p. 32 (inset) Lucky Business/Shutterstock.com; p. 33 pistol-seven/Shutterstock.com; p. 36 Jupiterimages/Comstock/Thinkstock; pp. 40–41 courtesy Rhode Island School of Design; p. 42 (inset) © iStockphoto.com/garymilner; p. 43 © Chang Jeong; p. 45 michaeljung /Shutterstock.com; pp. 48–49 Hero Images/Lifesize/Getty Images; pp. 50–51 Jacqueline Bohnert/The New York Times/Redux; cover and interior pages background patterns and graphics © iStockphoto.com/Ali Mazraie Shadi, © iStockphoto.com/MISHA, © iStockphoto.com/Paul Hill, © iStockphoto.com/Charles Taylor, © iStockphoto.com/Daniel Halvorson, © iStockphoto.com/Jeffrey Sheldon; additional interior page design elements © iStockphoto .com/Lisa Thornberg (laptop pp. 4, 13, 23, 32, 42), © iStockphoto .com/abu (computer mouse).

Editor: Andrea Sclarow Paskoff; Photo Researcher: Marty Levick